Racism

Origins, Impact, and the Path to Justice

By

Neil Potter

About the author

Neil Potter is a dedicated advocate for social justice, equality, and understanding. With a passion for unraveling the complexities of societal issues, Potter has delved into the intricate tapestry of racism, aiming to shed light on its origins, trace its impact through history, and chart a course toward a more just future.

Drawing from a diverse background in research, education, and community engagement, Potter brings a multidimensional perspective to the exploration of racism. His commitment to fostering dialogue and promoting awareness is reflected in his extensive work in anti-racist education and community-building initiatives.

Potter's journey into the heart of racial dynamics is not merely an academic pursuit; it's a personal mission rooted in the belief that knowledge, empathy, and collective action are essential tools in dismantling discriminatory systems. In "Racism: Origins, Impact, and the Path to Justice," Potter invites readers to join him on this transformative journey, encouraging reflection, dialogue, and, most importantly, a commitment to building a more inclusive and equitable world.

As an author, educator, and advocate, Neil Potter is dedicated to inspiring positive change, challenging ingrained biases, and contributing to the ongoing conversation about race and justice. Through his writing, he invites readers to be active participants in the pursuit of a society where every individual is treated with respect and dignity, irrespective of their race or ethnicity.

Appreciation

Dear Readers,

As I reflect on the journey of creating "Racism: Origins, Impact, and the Path to Justice," I am filled with gratitude for each of you who has taken the time to explore the pages of this book. This work is a culmination of passion, research, and a shared commitment to understanding and combating racism.

I appreciate your willingness to engage with the complexities of this crucial issue. It is through your curiosity, empathy, and dedication to knowledge that we collectively move toward a more just and equitable future. The exploration of racism requires courage, and I am grateful for the courage you've shown in joining this discourse.

To those who have shared their experiences, insights, and stories, your voices have added depth and nuance to this narrative. It is my hope that this book serves as a platform for continued dialogue, fostering a community of individuals committed to dismantling discriminatory systems.

Special appreciation goes to those who have been on the front lines of activism, advocacy, and education. Your tireless efforts inspire and drive positive change, reminding us all of the transformative power of collective action.

To my family, friends, and colleagues who have supported and encouraged this endeavor, your belief in the importance of this work has been a guiding light. Thank you for being steadfast companions on this journey.

As we turn the final pages of "Racism," let us carry forward the lessons learned, the empathy gained, and the commitment to justice. Our shared dedication is the catalyst for change, and together, we can contribute to the creation of a world where every individual is treated with respect, dignity, and equity.

With sincere appreciation,

Neil Potter

Copyright

Copyright © 2023 by Neil Potter

Dedication

To my Family,

You have been my unwavering source of love, support, and inspiration throughout this transformative journey. Your encouragement has fueled my commitment to understanding and combating racism, and your belief in the importance of this work has been a guiding force.

To my Parents, for instilling in me the values of empathy, justice, and the courage to confront difficult truths. Your wisdom and compassion have shaped the person I am today.

To my Siblings, for your constant encouragement, thoughtful discussions, and shared commitment to creating a more just world. Your perspectives have enriched my understanding and fueled my passion for this important cause.

To my Partner, for standing by me with unwavering support, patience, and understanding. Your love has been a driving force, reminding me of the profound impact we can have when we face societal challenges together.

This book is dedicated to each of you—the pillars of my life. Your love and support have made this journey not only possible but profoundly meaningful. May our collective efforts contribute to a future where justice, empathy, and equality prevail.

With love and gratitude,

Neil Potter

Table of contents

Racism

Introduction

Racism, a term that resonates with countless individuals across the world, represents a societal ill that has persisted through the ages. It has seeped into the very fabric of our communities, institutions, and cultures, perpetuating injustice and inequality. Understanding the origins of racism is paramount in addressing this complex and deeply rooted issue. This book embarks on a profound and illuminating journey, guided by the belief that to combat racism effectively, we must first trace its historical lineage, dissect its biological and psychological underpinnings, and scrutinize the socioeconomic and cultural dynamics that sustain it.

Throughout history, racism has thrived and mutated, taking on different forms in various epochs and regions. It is essential to place it within its historical context, examining the early human societies that laid the groundwork for racial distinctions. The age of exploration and colonialism, with its brutal subjugation of indigenous peoples, was a crucible for the growth of racial biases. The transatlantic slave trade, a dark chapter in human history, deepened the chasm of racial division.

Biological and psychological factors also play a pivotal role in the perpetuation of racism. Evolutionary perspectives on in-group bias and out-group discrimination offer insights into our primal instincts. Cognitive biases, such as confirmation bias and implicit prejudice, influence how we perceive and interact with those of different racial backgrounds. Social identity theory helps us understand how individuals derive their sense of self-worth from group affiliations, often leading to intergroup conflicts.

Moreover, socioeconomic factors, including economic disparities and social hierarchies, continue to fuel the fires of racism. The influence of power structures in shaping racial dynamics cannot be overstated. Discrimination persists, in part, because it serves the interests of dominant groups.

Cultural and ideological factors further propagate racism through stereotypes, historical ideologies, and pseudosciences. Media representation can either challenge or reinforce racial prejudices, depending on its portrayal of diverse communities.

Institutions, from government policies to educational systems and legal and justice systems, significantly impact the perpetuation or mitigation of racism. These institutions can either reinforce discriminatory practices or act as catalysts for change.

The book also delves into resistance and movements against racism, from historic civil rights movements to contemporary anti-racism activism. It acknowledges the progress made while highlighting the enduring challenges in the fight against racial discrimination.

In a world characterized by ongoing racial disparities and increasing recognition of intersectionality, this book provides a global perspective on racism. It calls upon us to envision a future where racism is no longer an insurmountable obstacle, where individuals from all racial backgrounds enjoy equal opportunities and treatment. We seek to explore the path forward, offering strategies to combat racism and fostering hope for a better future for all.

Join us on this intellectual journey as we confront the origins of racism, peel back the layers of this complex issue, and work toward a more just and equitable world for all its inhabitants.

Definition of racism

Racism is a deeply ingrained belief system and societal practice characterized by the belief in the inherent superiority of one racial group over others, leading to discrimination, prejudice, and the unequal treatment of individuals or groups based on their perceived racial or ethnic identity. It encompasses both individual attitudes and systemic structures that perpetuate racial disparities and injustices.

Importance of understanding its origins

Understanding the origins of racism is of paramount importance for several reasons:

- **Effective Mitigation:**

To combat racism effectively, it is crucial to address its root causes. By understanding where and how racism began, we can develop more informed and targeted strategies to dismantle it at its source.

- **Prevention:**

Knowledge of the origins can help prevent the resurgence of racism. By identifying the historical, cultural, and societal factors that gave rise to racism, we can work to prevent its reemergence in new forms or under different guises.

- **Promoting Empathy:**

Understanding the historical context and the factors that contributed to racism can foster empathy and better intergroup understanding. It allows individuals to appreciate the experiences of marginalized communities and recognize the harm caused by discriminatory practices.

- **Legal and Policy Reforms:**

Insights into the origins of racism can inform the reform of laws and policies. It can lead to the development of anti-discrimination legislation and affirmative action measures aimed at rectifying historical injustices.

- **Education and Awareness:**

Knowledge of the origins of racism can be integrated into educational curricula and public awareness campaigns. This can help educate future generations about the harmful consequences of racism and encourage a more inclusive society.

- ## **Healing and Reconciliation:**

In many cases, acknowledging and understanding the origins of racism is a crucial step in the process of healing and reconciliation for affected communities. It can pave the way for truth and reconciliation commissions or similar initiatives.

- ## **Social Change:**

Awareness of racism's origins can inspire and galvanize social change movements. It can serve as a catalyst for individuals and communities to advocate for racial justice, equality, and systemic reform.

- ## **Global Perspective:**

Racism is not confined to one region or time period. Understanding its origins on a global scale can promote international cooperation and solidarity in the fight against racism.

In sum, understanding the origins of racism is essential for addressing the issue comprehensively, promoting a more inclusive society, and working towards a future free from racial discrimination and inequality.

Overview of the book's approach

The approach of this book to uncover the origins of racism is multifaceted, comprehensive, and informed by both historical and contemporary perspectives. It draws upon a diverse range of disciplines and methods to provide a holistic understanding of the complex phenomenon of racism. Here is an overview of the book's approach:

- **Interdisciplinary Exploration:**

The book takes an interdisciplinary approach, weaving together insights from history, sociology, psychology, biology, economics, and other relevant fields. This broad perspective allows for a nuanced analysis of racism's origins.

- **Historical Context:**

It delves deeply into the historical roots of racism, examining pivotal events, periods, and civilizations where racial discrimination and prejudice began to take shape. This historical context helps to trace the evolution of racist ideologies and practices.

- **Biological and Psychological Insights:**

The book explores the biological and psychological factors that contribute to the development of racist attitudes and behaviors. It delves into evolutionary theories, cognitive biases, and social identity theory to provide a comprehensive understanding of the individual-level origins of racism.

- **Socioeconomic Factors:**

It analyzes the role of economic disparities, social hierarchies, and power structures in perpetuating racism. These factors are explored in relation to the historical and contemporary dimensions of racism.

- ## **Cultural and Ideological Factors:**

The book investigates how cultural stereotypes, historical ideologies, and pseudosciences have been used to justify and sustain racist beliefs and practices. It also explores the impact of media representation in shaping public perceptions of different racial and ethnic groups.

- ## **Institutional Influence:**

It scrutinizes how various institutions, including government policies, educational systems, and legal and justice systems, play a significant role in perpetuating or mitigating racism. The impact of these institutions on racial disparities is a central focus.

- ## **Resistance and Movements:**

The book highlights the history of resistance to racism, including civil rights movements and contemporary anti-racism activism. It showcases the achievements and ongoing challenges faced by those working to combat racism.

- **Global Perspective:**

The book takes a global perspective, recognizing that racism is not confined to a specific region or culture. It explores the manifestations and consequences of racism on a global scale, acknowledging the interconnectedness of racial issues.

- **Call to Action:**

Throughout the book, there is a strong emphasis on a call to action. It encourages readers to critically engage with the material presented, reflect on their own beliefs and behaviors, and become agents of change in the fight against racism.

By adopting this comprehensive and multidisciplinary approach, the book aims to provide readers with a deep and holistic understanding of the origins of racism, equipping them with the knowledge and insight needed to actively contribute to the ongoing struggle for a more just and equitable world.

Chapter One: Historical Context

Racism, as a deeply ingrained belief system and practice, has a long and complex history. Understanding its origins requires a look back at key historical events and developments that laid the groundwork for racial discrimination and prejudice. The historical context can be summarized in several key periods and factors:

- **Early Human Societies:**

Racial distinctions can be traced back to early human societies, where different groups often defined themselves in opposition to others. These distinctions were often based on physical differences, geographic location, or cultural practices. However, these early distinctions were not necessarily based on the same racial categories that exist today.

- ## Age of Exploration and Colonialism:

The European age of exploration and subsequent colonial expansion in the 15th to 19th centuries marked a significant turning point. European powers began to subjugate indigenous populations in various parts of the world, asserting the superiority of their own culture and race. The concept of racial hierarchy and the idea of a "civilized" European race in contrast to "savage" or "inferior" indigenous peoples emerged.

- ## Transatlantic Slave Trade:

The transatlantic slave trade, from the 16th to the 19th centuries, was a pivotal moment in the development of racism. Millions of Africans were forcibly taken from their homelands and enslaved in the Americas. Racist ideologies were constructed to justify this inhumane practice, portraying Africans as inferior and deserving of enslavement.

- **Scientific Racism:**

In the 18th and 19th centuries, the pseudoscience of "scientific racism" emerged, using selective interpretations of biology and anthropology to support racist ideas. This included the categorization of human races, with Europeans often positioned at the top of the hierarchy.

- **Colonial Legacies:**

The colonial legacy of racial divisions persisted even after the end of formal colonial rule. Many countries continued to grapple with racial inequalities and discrimination, often codified in laws and social structures.

- **Civil Rights Movements:**

The mid-20th century saw the rise of civil rights movements in response to deeply entrenched racism, particularly in the United States. These movements sought to challenge racial segregation, discrimination, and injustice.

Understanding this historical context is essential in comprehending the origins of racism. It reveals the evolution of racial hierarchies, the use of racial ideologies to justify exploitation, and the enduring impact of these historical events on contemporary racial dynamics. Racism, therefore, cannot be divorced from its historical roots, and its legacy continues to shape our world today.

Early human societies

Early human societies provide important insights into the origins of racial distinctions and the development of human social structures. While it's important to note that early human societies did not conceive of race in the same way modern societies do, there were still factors that contributed to the formation of group identities and distinctions. Here are some key points regarding early human societies:

- **Hunter-Gatherer Communities:**

Early human societies were primarily hunter-gatherer communities. These groups often formed along familial or tribal lines, with a strong sense of kinship and shared identity.

- **Physical Differences:**

Physical differences, such as skin color, facial features, and body size, were readily apparent among different groups of early humans. These variations were often linked to geographic locations and environmental adaptations.

- **Ethnic and Cultural Distinctions:**

Early humans developed distinct ethnic and cultural identities based on their environments, practices, and beliefs. These identities were not necessarily racial but rather centered around the customs and traditions of each group.

- **Competition for Resources:**

Groups often competed for limited resources like food, water, and shelter. This competition could lead to intergroup conflicts and tensions.

- **In-Group and Out-Group Dynamics:**

Early humans typically had strong in-group bonds and were often wary of outsiders. This natural tendency to form close-knit communities and be cautious of those who appeared different played a role in the development of social divisions.

- **Language and Communication:**

Language and communication were vital for early human societies. Language differences could serve as markers of group identity and affiliation.

- **Cultural Practices:**

Different groups developed unique cultural practices, such as clothing, body ornamentation, and art. These practices reinforced a sense of belonging within the group.

It's important to emphasize that early human societies did not have the same concept of race as we do today. The racial categories and hierarchies that have been constructed over time are modern social constructs. However, the processes of group formation, identity, and interaction in early human societies laid the foundation for how humans would later perceive and interact with individuals from other groups. Understanding these early dynamics helps to trace the origins of social divisions and prejudices based on perceived differences.

Exploration and colonialism

The age of exploration and colonialism, which spanned from the late 15th century to the 19th century, marked a transformative period in human history. It significantly contributed to the development of racism and racial hierarchies. Here's an overview of this historical context:

Exploration and Colonialism

- **European Expansion:**

European powers, primarily Spain and Portugal in the early stages, embarked on ambitious exploration and expansion ventures. They sought new trade routes, resources, and territories to establish empires.

- **Subjugation of Indigenous Peoples:**

As European explorers reached new lands, they encountered indigenous populations in

Africa, the Americas, Asia, and other regions. Many indigenous cultures were subjugated and displaced through force, coercion, and disease. The idea of European superiority over these indigenous groups began to emerge.

- **Racial Hierarchies:**

The European colonial powers started to construct racial hierarchies, positioning themselves as superior to indigenous peoples. This ideological framework served to justify the exploitation and enslavement of indigenous populations.

- **Transatlantic Slave Trade:**

The transatlantic slave trade was a central element of this period. Millions of Africans were forcibly transported to the Americas as slaves. The racist ideology portrayed Africans as inferior and thus deserving of enslavement. This period saw the dehumanization and brutal treatment of enslaved individuals.

- **Scientific Racism:**

In the 18th and 19th centuries, "scientific racism" emerged as a pseudoscientific attempt to justify racial hierarchies. Biologists, anthropologists, and others used selective interpretations of biology and anthropology to support the notion of European racial superiority.

- **Impact on Indigenous Cultures:**

Colonialism had devastating effects on indigenous cultures, leading to cultural assimilation, loss of languages and traditions, and significant population decline due to disease and conflict.

- **Codification of Racial Discrimination:**

Over time, colonial powers codified racial discrimination in their laws and systems of governance. Discriminatory practices, such as segregation and restrictions on the rights of non-European populations, were institutionalized.

- **Legacy of Colonialism:**

The legacy of colonialism is still felt in many parts of the world. It has left a lasting impact on racial dynamics, socioeconomic disparities, and political structures.

The age of exploration and colonialism was a pivotal period in the development of racism. The construction of racial hierarchies, the exploitation of indigenous peoples, and the transatlantic slave trade were central to this historical context. These events laid the foundation for later racial ideologies and systems of discrimination that continue to influence the world today. Understanding this history is essential for comprehending the origins of racial prejudice and discrimination.

Transatlantic slave trade

The transatlantic slave trade was a dark and deeply impactful chapter in human history that significantly contributed to the development of racism. Here is an overview of this historical phenomenon:

Transatlantic Slave Trade

- **Origins and Scope:**

The transatlantic slave trade, also known as the Atlantic slave trade, began in the late 15th century and continued for over four centuries, with its peak in the 18th century. It involved the forced capture, transportation, and enslavement of millions of Africans to the Americas, primarily to work on European colonies and plantations.

- **Triangular Trade:**

The trade operated in a triangular pattern. European ships carried manufactured goods (such as firearms, textiles, and alcohol) to Africa in exchange for enslaved Africans. These Africans were then transported to the Americas, where they were sold as slaves. The profits from the sale of enslaved individuals were used to purchase raw materials, primarily agricultural products like sugar, tobacco, and cotton, which were then shipped back to Europe.

- **Conditions of the Middle Passage:**

The journey across the Atlantic, known as the Middle Passage, was characterized by horrific conditions. Enslaved Africans endured overcrowded and unsanitary conditions, malnutrition, disease, and extreme brutality. Many did not survive the voyage.

- **Dehumanization:**

The transatlantic slave trade was underpinned by a dehumanizing ideology. Enslaved Africans were viewed as property rather than as human beings. Racist ideologies emerged to rationalize their enslavement, portraying Africans as inferior and deserving of their fate.

- **Impact on African Societies:**

The slave trade had a devastating impact on African societies. It led to the depopulation of certain regions, disrupted local economies, and caused social and political upheaval. Some African leaders and traders were complicit in the trade, while others resisted it.

- **Labor on Plantations:**

Enslaved Africans were forced to work on European-owned plantations in the

Americas, primarily in regions like the Caribbean, South America, and the southern United States. They provided the labor force essential for the production of cash crops like sugar, tobacco, and cotton.

- ## **Cultural Impact:**

Enslaved Africans brought their cultures, languages, and traditions to the Americas, influencing the development of African diaspora cultures that persist today.

- ## **Abolition Movements:**

The transatlantic slave trade was eventually met with significant opposition. Abolitionist movements in Europe and the Americas called for the end of the trade and the emancipation of enslaved individuals.

- **End of the Trade:**

The transatlantic slave trade began to decline in the 19th century and was officially abolished in most European countries in the early 19th century. The United States abolished the international slave trade in 1808.

- **Legacy:**

The legacy of the transatlantic slave trade endures, with long-lasting effects on racial dynamics, socioeconomic disparities, and cultural identities in the Americas and Europe. It played a pivotal role in the development of racial prejudice and systemic racism.

Understanding the transatlantic slave trade is essential for comprehending the historical roots of racial discrimination, as it was a major catalyst for the construction of racial hierarchies and the development of racist ideologies.

Chapter Two: Biological and Psychological Factors

Biological and psychological factors play a significant role in understanding the origins of racism. These factors help shed light on why individuals may hold racist beliefs or exhibit discriminatory behaviors. Here's an overview of the key elements in this context:

Biological Factors

- **Evolutionary Perspectives:**

Some scholars have explored the evolutionary basis of in-group favoritism and out-group bias. These behaviors may have provided an adaptive advantage to early human groups by fostering cooperation within the group. However, this natural inclination to favor one's own group can lead to discrimination when applied to racial or ethnic groups perceived as different.

- ## **Cognitive Biases:**

Cognitive biases, such as confirmation bias, in-group bias, and out-group derogation, can contribute to the development of racist attitudes. People tend to seek information that confirms their existing beliefs and may hold negative stereotypes about out-groups, which can lead to prejudice.

- ## **Implicit Bias:**

Implicit bias refers to the unconscious and automatic biases that people hold, often without being aware of them. Research has shown that many individuals may have implicit biases related to race, even if they consciously reject racism. These biases can influence decision-making and behavior.

Psychological Factors

1. **Social Identity Theory:**

Social identity theory posits that individuals derive their sense of self-worth from their group affiliations. This can lead to intergroup competition and bias, as people seek to maintain a positive social identity by favoring their in-group and discriminating against out-groups.

2. **Social Learning:**

Racism can be learned through socialization and exposure to prejudiced attitudes and behaviors within families, communities, and society at large. Children often absorb racial stereotypes from their environment.

3. **Stereotyping and Prejudice:**

Stereotyping is a cognitive process that categorizes individuals into groups based on perceived characteristics. Prejudice refers to the negative attitudes and emotions associated with these stereotypes. Both stereotyping and prejudice are key psychological factors contributing to racism.

4. **Authoritarianism:**

Some psychological studies have explored the link between authoritarian personality traits and racist attitudes. Authoritarians tend to be rigid in their thinking, intolerant of ambiguity, and prone to accepting social hierarchies.

5. **Contact Hypothesis:**

The contact hypothesis suggests that intergroup contact under positive conditions can reduce prejudice. However, this effect depends on factors such as equal status, common goals, and cooperative interaction between groups.

6. **Psychological Defense Mechanisms:**

Individuals may use psychological defense mechanisms, such as projection, displacement, or scapegoating, to deal with anxiety and insecurities related to perceived threats from other racial or ethnic groups.

These mechanisms can lead to discriminatory behaviors.

Understanding these biological and psychological factors is crucial for comprehending how racism is not solely a societal issue but also deeply embedded in human cognition and behavior. It highlights the importance of addressing these factors in efforts to combat racism and promote intergroup understanding and equality.

Evolutionary perspectives

Evolutionary perspectives on the origins of racism suggest that certain behaviors and biases related to in-group favoritism and out-group bias have deep-seated roots in human evolution. While it's important to note that evolutionary theories do not excuse or justify racism, they offer insights into the possible origins of these behaviors. Here are some key points related to evolutionary perspectives:

- **In-Group Favoritism:**

Evolutionary psychology proposes that humans have evolved to favor members of their own group, or "in-group," over members of other groups, or "out-groups." This preference for the in-group could have provided an adaptive advantage by promoting cooperation, mutual support, and a sense of belonging within the group. In a hunter-gatherer context, these bonds may have been critical for survival.

- **Out-Group Suspicion:**

Evolutionary perspectives also suggest that humans may have developed a natural wariness or suspicion of individuals from different groups, which could have served as a defense mechanism in the ancestral environment. Being cautious of outsiders may have helped protect the group from potential threats.

- **Formation of Social Hierarchies:**

Evolutionary theories propose that the tendency to form social hierarchies may have roots in early human societies. Hierarchies can lead to the unequal treatment of individuals or groups, which, in a modern context, can contribute to racism.

- **Resource Competition:**

Competition for limited resources, such as food, territory, or mates, may have intensified intergroup conflict and the development of biases against perceived rivals. This competition could have contributed to the emergence of group-based prejudices.

- **Biological Foundations:**

Some researchers suggest that certain biological factors, such as hormones like testosterone, may influence the expression of these evolutionary behaviors. High levels of testosterone have been linked to increased aggression and dominance, which could play a role in intergroup conflicts.

It's essential to emphasize that these evolutionary perspectives provide a framework for understanding potential origins of behaviors related to racism, but they do not justify or condone racist attitudes or actions. Modern societies strive to overcome these innate biases and promote tolerance, diversity, and inclusivity.

Furthermore, contemporary human societies are characterized by complex cultural, social, and ethical considerations that can mitigate or amplify these evolutionary tendencies. Understanding these perspectives helps us acknowledge the cognitive biases that may contribute to racism and underscores the importance of education, socialization, and efforts to promote equality and social cohesion.

Cognitive biases and prejudice

Cognitive biases and prejudice are interconnected and can significantly influence the development of racist attitudes and behaviors. Cognitive biases are systematic patterns of deviation from norm or rationality in judgment, often leading to perceptual distortion and inaccurate judgment. Prejudice, on the other hand, refers to preconceived opinions or attitudes, usually unfavorable, held about individuals or groups. Here's how cognitive biases and prejudice relate to the origin of racism:

1. Confirmation Bias

This cognitive bias involves seeking out information that confirms one's existing beliefs while ignoring or dismissing information that contradicts those beliefs. In the context of racism, individuals with prejudiced attitudes may selectively interpret and remember information that supports their biases, thereby reinforcing their discriminatory beliefs.

2. In-Group Bias:

In-group bias is a cognitive bias where individuals favor members of their own group (the in-group) over members of other groups (the out-group). This bias can lead to favoritism and positive attitudes toward one's own racial or ethnic group while displaying prejudice and negative attitudes toward out-groups.

3. Out-Group Homogeneity:

This bias involves perceiving members of an out-group as more homogeneous or similar to each other than they actually are. It can contribute to stereotypes and prejudices because people may assume that all members of an out-group share the same negative traits or characteristics.

4. Stereotyping:

Stereotyping is a cognitive process that involves categorizing individuals into groups based on perceived characteristics or traits. Stereotypes can be based on race, ethnicity, or other group attributes and often result in generalizations and oversimplifications, leading to prejudiced attitudes.

5. Implicit Bias:

Implicit bias refers to unconscious biases or attitudes that people may hold without being consciously aware of them. Research has shown that implicit biases related to race can influence behavior and decisions, even among individuals who consciously reject racism.

6. Contact Hypothesis:

While not a cognitive bias per se, the contact hypothesis suggests that positive interactions between members of different groups can reduce prejudice. However, cognitive biases like in-group bias and out-group homogeneity can impact the success of intergroup contact in reducing prejudice.

7. Attribution Errors:

People often make attribution errors when explaining the behavior of individuals from different racial or ethnic backgrounds. For example, they may attribute negative behavior by an out-group member to internal characteristics (e.g., personality) rather than external factors (e.g., the situation). This can lead to biased judgments and prejudice.

Understanding how cognitive biases interact with prejudice is crucial for comprehending the development and persistence of racism. These biases can lead to prejudiced beliefs, discriminatory actions, and the perpetuation of stereotypes. Combatting racism involves recognizing and challenging these biases through education, awareness, and conscious efforts to promote equality and intergroup understanding.

Social identity theory

Social identity theory is a psychological framework that helps explain how individuals derive their sense of self-worth and identity from their group affiliations. It offers insights into the development of in-group favoritism, out-group bias, and intergroup conflicts, which are relevant to understanding the origins of racism. Here are the key principles of social identity theory:

- **Categorization:**

Social identity theory proposes that individuals categorize themselves and others into various social groups based on shared characteristics. These characteristics can include race, ethnicity, nationality, religion, gender, or any other attribute that leads to group identification.

- ## **Identification:**

People not only categorize themselves but also identify with these groups. They see themselves as members of these social categories and derive a sense of self-worth and identity from their group memberships.

- ## **In-Group Favoritism:**

Social identity theory suggests that individuals tend to favor and show more positive attitudes toward their in-group, the group with which they identify. This in-group favoritism can lead to a preference for one's own racial or ethnic group, contributing to discriminatory attitudes and behaviors toward out-groups.

- ## **Out-Group Bias:**

In parallel with in-group favoritism, individuals may also display out-group bias, which involves negative attitudes and behaviors toward members of groups to which they do not belong. This can manifest as prejudice and discrimination.

• **Social Comparison:**

Individuals engage in social comparison to enhance their self-esteem. They may compare their own group with other groups, and when their group is perceived as superior, this can boost their self-esteem. Conversely, when their group is perceived as inferior, this can lead to feelings of insecurity.

• **Intergroup Conflict:**

Social identity theory explains that intergroup conflict arises when individuals perceive their in-group as being threatened or inferior to out-groups. In response to this perceived threat, they may engage in discriminatory behavior to maintain a positive social identity.

- **Self-Categorization:**

The theory also highlights the role of self-categorization, which refers to the flexibility of an individual's identity. People can shift their identity to be more inclusive (e.g., as part of a broader human race) or more exclusive (e.g., identifying primarily with a specific nationality or ethnicity) depending on the context and their goals.

Understanding social identity theory is essential in comprehending how individuals form and maintain their identities in a social context, and how this process can lead to biases, prejudices, and discrimination. Addressing racism and promoting intergroup harmony often involves challenging and expanding individuals' social identities to encompass a broader sense of humanity and shared values.

Chapter Three: Socioeconomic Factors

Socioeconomic factors play a significant role in understanding the origins of racism. These factors relate to the influence of economic disparities, social hierarchies, and power structures in shaping racial dynamics. Here are the key elements of how socioeconomic factors contribute to the development of racism:

- **Economic Disparities:**

Economic disparities between racial or ethnic groups are a prominent aspect of racism. Historically, many minority racial and ethnic groups have faced systemic economic disadvantages, including limited access to quality education, employment discrimination, and unequal economic opportunities. These disparities contribute to the perpetuation of racism as they reinforce the idea that certain racial groups are inferior or undeserving of economic success.

- ## **Social Hierarchies:**

Societies often establish social hierarchies based on race, where certain racial or ethnic groups are granted higher social status and privilege, while others are marginalized and oppressed. These hierarchies create and perpetuate racial discrimination and inequality.

- ## **Power Structures:**

Power structures within societies, including political, legal, and economic systems, can be manipulated to maintain racial hierarchies. When individuals from dominant racial groups hold positions of power, they may enact policies and practices that favor their own group while disadvantaging others, leading to racial disparities and reinforcing racism.

- ## **Employment Discrimination:**

Racism can manifest in employment discrimination, where individuals from certain racial groups face barriers to accessing and advancing in the job market. This discrimination can lead to reduced opportunities, lower income levels, and economic inequality, perpetuating racial divisions.

- **Education Disparities:**

Unequal access to quality education is a socioeconomic factor that contributes to racism. When minority racial groups have limited access to quality schools and educational resources, it hinders their social mobility and perpetuates cycles of poverty and inequality.

- **Housing Segregation:**

Socioeconomic factors are intertwined with housing segregation, which has been historically enforced through policies and practices that restricted where individuals from different racial groups could live. This segregation contributes to the development of racially segregated communities with disparities in access to resources and opportunities.

- **Wealth Disparities:**

Wealth disparities often align with racial disparities, with minority racial groups generally having less accumulated wealth and assets. These disparities are often intergenerational, as historical injustices continue to impact the economic well-being of racial minority communities.

- **Criminal Justice System:**

Socioeconomic factors are closely linked to racial disparities in the criminal justice system. Racial minorities, particularly African Americans and Hispanic individuals, are disproportionately represented in the criminal justice system, facing higher rates of arrest, incarceration, and harsh sentencing.

Understanding these socioeconomic factors is crucial in comprehending how racism operates within societies. It highlights the systemic and structural nature of racism and the need for systemic change to address and rectify these disparities. Efforts to combat racism often involve policy reforms, affirmative action measures, and initiatives aimed at reducing economic and social inequalities based on race.

Economic disparities

Economic disparities are significant factors contributing to the origins and perpetuation of racism. These disparities represent inequalities in income, wealth, employment opportunities, and access to economic resources between racial or ethnic groups. Here are some key points related to economic disparities and their role in racism:

- **Historical Injustices:**

Many racial and ethnic groups have faced historical injustices, such as slavery, colonization, and forced labor, which have had enduring economic repercussions. The legacies of these injustices continue to contribute to economic disparities between racial groups.

- **Access to Education:**

Unequal access to quality education is a critical factor in economic disparities.

Minority racial and ethnic groups often have limited access to quality schools and educational resources, which can hinder their economic opportunities and income potential.

- **Employment Discrimination:**

Employment discrimination, both overt and subtle, continues to be a significant issue. Racial minorities may face biases in hiring, promotion, and wages, leading to disparities in income and career advancement.

- **Wage Gap:**

Racial wage gaps persist, with individuals from minority racial groups typically earning less than their white counterparts for the same work. This wage gap is a key indicator of economic disparities driven by racism.

- ## **Wealth Disparities:**

Wealth disparities represent the difference in accumulated assets, including property, investments, and savings. Minority racial groups often have significantly less accumulated wealth than white individuals and families, which limits their economic stability and opportunities.

- ## **Housing Segregation:**

Economic disparities are linked to housing segregation, which can limit access to quality neighborhoods, schools, and job opportunities. Housing policies and practices that perpetuate segregation contribute to unequal economic outcomes.

- ## **Entrepreneurship and Business Ownership:**

Minority individuals may face barriers to entrepreneurship and business ownership due to limited access to capital, resources, and markets. These barriers can result in disparities in business ownership and economic self-sufficiency.

- **Financial Services:**

Access to financial services, including loans and banking, can be more limited for minority communities, making it challenging to build wealth and access economic opportunities.

- **Criminal Justice System:**

Racial disparities in the criminal justice system can have economic consequences. Convictions and incarceration can lead to job loss, reduced income, and limited economic mobility.

- **Economic Mobility:**

Limited economic mobility for minority communities can result in generational poverty, making it difficult for individuals and families to break free from the cycle of economic disparities.

Addressing economic disparities is a central focus in efforts to combat racism. This involves policy reforms, such as affirmative action measures, anti-discrimination legislation, and initiatives aimed at improving educational and employment opportunities for racial minority groups. Reducing economic disparities is a critical step in promoting equality and social justice.

Social hierarchies and classism

Social hierarchies and classism are closely related to the origins and perpetuation of racism, as they reflect broader systems of inequality and discrimination. Here's an overview of how social hierarchies and classism intersect with racism:

Social Hierarchies:

- **Racial Hierarchies:**

Social hierarchies often involve the ranking of racial or ethnic groups based on perceived superiority or inferiority. Historically, these hierarchies have been used to justify the exploitation and oppression of racial minority groups, such as African Americans, Indigenous peoples, and other marginalized communities.

- **Power Dynamics:**

Social hierarchies are characterized by power imbalances, with dominant racial groups holding more societal power and privilege. This power can be used to maintain and reinforce racial discrimination.

• Cultural and Economic Capital:

Social hierarchies are closely tied to the distribution of cultural and economic capital. Dominant racial groups have historically had greater access to education, employment opportunities, and economic resources, while marginalized groups have faced barriers to accessing these benefits.

• Legal and Political Structures:

Social hierarchies are often reinforced and perpetuated through legal and political systems. Laws and policies may favor dominant racial groups, while discriminating against racial minority groups. For example, historical segregation laws in the United States enforced racial hierarchies.

Classism:

- **Class-Based Discrimination:**

Classism is discrimination based on socioeconomic class. It can intersect with racism when individuals from racial minority groups also face economic disadvantages. This double burden can lead to compounded discrimination and further marginalization.

- **Economic Inequality:**

Classism is intertwined with economic inequality. Racial minority groups often face economic disparities due to historical injustices and ongoing discrimination. Classism reinforces these disparities by perpetuating unequal access to economic resources.

- **Access to Education:**

Class-based discrimination can manifest in unequal access to quality education, which has a profound impact on economic opportunities. Racial minority communities often have limited access to quality schools, exacerbating class-based disparities.

- **Housing Disparities:**

Classism is evident in housing disparities, where individuals with lower socioeconomic status often face limited access to safe and affordable housing. This can be compounded by racial discrimination in housing markets.

- **Employment Discrimination:**

Classism is closely linked to employment discrimination, as individuals from lower socioeconomic classes often face barriers to job opportunities and career advancement. Racial minority groups experiencing both racism and classism may face particularly significant challenges in the job market.

- **Healthcare Disparities:**

Class-based discrimination is reflected in healthcare disparities, where individuals with lower socioeconomic status may have limited access to quality healthcare. Racial disparities in healthcare outcomes can intersect with classism, leading to compounded health inequities.

Efforts to combat racism must also address social hierarchies and classism. This involves advocating for economic equality, access to quality education, and policies that address both racial and socioeconomic disparities. Recognizing the intersections of race and class is essential for understanding the complexity of discrimination and working toward a more equitable society.

Power structures

Power structures are fundamental to understanding the origins and perpetuation of racism. These structures encompass political, economic, social, and cultural systems that influence and maintain racial hierarchies. Here are key aspects of how power structures relate to racism:

- **Political Power:**

Political power plays a central role in the development and perpetuation of racism. Governments and political institutions have historically been used to enact policies that discriminate against racial minority groups. Examples include segregation laws, voter suppression, and racially biased criminal justice policies.

- **Legal Systems:**

Legal systems within societies can reinforce and perpetuate racial discrimination. Historical laws, such as Jim Crow laws in the United States, codified racial segregation and inequality. Even after legal changes, racial bias can persist within legal systems, affecting sentencing, policing, and access to justice.

- **Economic Structures:**

Economic power structures can result in disparities between racial groups. Economic inequality is often perpetuated through discriminatory practices in employment, housing, and financial services. Racial minorities may have limited access to economic resources and opportunities, which can reinforce racial hierarchies.

- **Media and Representation:**

Media and cultural institutions have the power to shape public perception and influence attitudes toward race. Stereotypical or biased portrayals of racial minority groups in media can contribute to prejudice and discrimination. In contrast, media can also be a powerful tool for challenging racism and promoting awareness.

- **Education Systems:**

Education systems can either challenge or perpetuate racism. Unequal access to quality education can limit opportunities for racial minority groups. Curriculum choices, teacher bias, and disciplinary practices can also play a role in perpetuating racial disparities in education.

- **Social and Cultural Norms:**

Social norms and cultural values are embedded in power structures and can influence attitudes and behaviors related to race. Dominant racial groups may shape societal norms that favor their own group, while marginalized racial groups are excluded or stigmatized.

- **Language and Rhetoric:**

The language used by individuals in positions of power, including politicians and leaders, can have a significant impact on shaping public perceptions of race. Racist rhetoric or dog whistles can be used to exploit and manipulate racial fears and prejudices.

- **Institutional Discrimination:**

Discrimination within institutions, such as government agencies, corporations, and nonprofit organizations, can perpetuate racism. This includes discriminatory hiring practices, unequal opportunities for advancement, and a lack of diversity in leadership roles.

Understanding power structures is essential for recognizing how systemic racism operates within societies. Addressing racism often involves challenging these structures and advocating for policies and practices that promote equality, diversity, and social justice. Recognizing the ways in which power is used to maintain racial hierarchies is a critical step in working toward a more inclusive and equitable society.

Chapter Four: Cultural and Ideological Factors

Cultural and ideological factors play a significant role in the origins and perpetuation of racism. These factors involve the beliefs, values, norms, and narratives that shape societal attitudes and behaviors related to race. Here are key elements related to cultural and ideological factors in racism:

1. Stereotypes and Prejudice:

Cultural factors contribute to the creation and perpetuation of racial stereotypes. These stereotypes are often negative and can lead to prejudiced attitudes and discriminatory behavior toward individuals from racial minority groups.

2. Socialization:

Individuals are socialized into cultural norms and beliefs about race from an early age. This socialization can occur within families, communities, educational institutions, and media. Cultural narratives about racial superiority and inferiority can be passed down through generations.

3. Media Portrayals:

Cultural factors are reflected in media portrayals of race and ethnicity. Biased or stereotypical representations in film, television, and other media can reinforce racial prejudice and discrimination.

4. Language and Terminology:

Cultural factors influence the language and terminology used to discuss race. The choice of words and the way racial groups are described can perpetuate harmful stereotypes and contribute to the normalization of racism.

5. Myths and Narratives:

Cultural myths and narratives often shape beliefs about race. For example, the myth of racial purity has been used to justify discrimination and segregation. Ideological narratives that portray certain racial groups as threats or as inferior can fuel racial prejudice.

6. Colorism:

Cultural factors also contribute to colorism, which is discrimination or bias based on skin color within racial groups. Lighter skin tones are often privileged over darker skin tones, reflecting deeply ingrained cultural values and biases.

7. Cultural Appropriation:

Cultural factors can manifest as cultural appropriation, where elements of one culture are adopted or borrowed by members of another culture. This can lead to the commodification and exploitation of aspects of racial and ethnic identities.

8. Racial Superiority Ideologies:

Ideological factors may involve beliefs in racial superiority and supremacy. These ideologies often result in the devaluation and discrimination against individuals from racial minority groups.

9. Racial Essentialism:

Ideological factors can also include the belief in racial essentialism, which sees racial groups as having fixed and unchangeable characteristics. This perspective can lead to prejudiced attitudes and discriminatory behavior.

Understanding cultural and ideological factors in racism is essential for addressing its root causes. Efforts to combat racism often involve challenging and changing cultural narratives, promoting diversity and inclusion, and educating individuals and communities about the harmful impact of stereotypes and biases. By challenging these cultural and ideological factors, societies can work toward a more inclusive and equitable future.

Cultural stereotypes

Cultural stereotypes are oversimplified beliefs or assumptions about the characteristics, behaviors, and attributes of individuals from specific cultural or ethnic groups. These stereotypes often arise from cultural misunderstandings, limited exposure to other cultures, or the perpetuation of biased and discriminatory narratives. Here are some common examples of cultural stereotypes and their impact:

- **Asian Stereotype:**

The "model minority" stereotype often portrays Asian individuals as exceptionally successful academically and economically. While it may seem positive, this stereotype can be harmful as it ignores the diversity within Asian communities and creates unrealistic expectations.

- **Black Stereotype:**

Stereotypes about Black individuals can be negative and include assumptions about criminality, laziness, or lack of intelligence. These stereotypes have deep historical roots and have contributed to systemic racism.

- **Latino Stereotype:**

Latino stereotypes can include assumptions about immigration status, criminal activity, or limited education. These stereotypes perpetuate discrimination and can negatively impact opportunities for Latino individuals.

- **Native American Stereotype:**

Stereotypes about Native Americans often involve outdated and inaccurate portrayals of "savagery" or a romanticized view of Indigenous culture. These stereotypes perpetuate ignorance and discrimination.

- **Middle Eastern Stereotype:**

Stereotypes about people from the Middle East often center around terrorism, violence, or religious extremism. These stereotypes contribute to discrimination, particularly in the context of Islamophobia.

- **Gender and Cultural Stereotypes:**

Stereotypes related to both gender and culture can intersect. For example, the stereotype that women from certain cultural backgrounds are submissive or oppressed can lead to further marginalization and discrimination.

Impact of Cultural Stereotypes:

- **Discrimination:**

Cultural stereotypes can lead to discrimination in various aspects of life, including employment, housing, education, and social interactions.

- **Reduced Opportunities:**

When individuals are judged based on stereotypes rather than their individual merits, they may face limited opportunities and have to work harder to overcome biased perceptions.

- **Mental and Emotional Harm:**

The perpetuation of stereotypes can harm the mental and emotional well-being of those targeted, leading to feelings of isolation, stress, and a sense of not belonging.

- **Reinforcement of Prejudice:**

Cultural stereotypes can reinforce broader prejudices and contribute to systemic racism and discrimination.

Combating Cultural Stereotypes:

- **Education:**

Raising awareness and educating individuals about the harm of stereotypes is essential. This includes teaching critical thinking skills and promoting cultural competence.

- **Diverse Representation:**

Promoting accurate and diverse portrayals of individuals from different cultural backgrounds in media, literature, and other forms of communication can help challenge stereotypes.

- **Community Dialogue:**

Encouraging open and respectful dialogues about cultural differences and stereotypes within communities can foster understanding and empathy.

- **Legislation:**

Legal measures can be put in place to combat discrimination based on cultural stereotypes. Anti-discrimination laws and policies are important in this regard.

Recognizing and challenging cultural stereotypes is a crucial step in addressing racism and promoting a more inclusive and equitable society.

Historical ideologies and pseudosciences

Historical ideologies and pseudosciences have played a significant role in shaping racist beliefs and practices throughout history. These flawed theories and ideologies were used to justify discrimination, oppression, and violence against various racial and ethnic groups. Here are some key historical ideologies and pseudosciences related to racism:

- **Scientific Racism:**

Scientific racism was a pseudoscientific ideology that emerged in the 18th and 19th centuries. It claimed that there were inherent biological and intellectual differences between racial groups, with a hierarchy that positioned white Europeans as superior and other racial groups as inferior. These ideas were used to justify colonialism, slavery, and discrimination.

• **Social Darwinism:**

Social Darwinism drew on Charles Darwin's theory of natural selection to argue that social and economic inequalities were the result of natural competition, with some races and societies seen as more "fit" than others. This ideology was used to rationalize imperialism and the domination of non-European societies.

• **Eugenics:**

Eugenics was a movement that aimed to improve the genetic quality of the human population by promoting selective breeding. It led to policies of forced sterilization and, in some cases, euthanasia, targeting individuals deemed "genetically undesirable." Eugenics often targeted minority racial and ethnic groups, such as African Americans and Indigenous peoples.

- **Phrenology:**

Phrenology was a pseudoscience that claimed to determine a person's mental and moral attributes by examining the shape and size of their skull. It was used to support racial stereotypes and prejudices, as well as to justify discriminatory practices.

- **White Supremacy:**

White supremacy is an ideology that asserts the inherent superiority of white people over other racial groups. This ideology has been used to justify colonialism, slavery, segregation, and various forms of racial discrimination.

- **Aryan Supremacy:**

Aryan supremacy was a central tenet of Nazi ideology, asserting the superiority of the "Aryan race" and promoting the persecution and extermination of Jews and other minority groups during the Holocaust.

- **Anti-Miscegenation Laws:**

Many regions had laws prohibiting interracial marriage, known as anti-miscegenation laws. These laws were based on the idea that racial mixing would lead to the degradation of the "superior" race.

- **Segregation:**

Segregation laws, particularly in the United States, enforced the separation of racial groups in public facilities, schools, and housing. These laws institutionalized racial discrimination and inequality.

- **Colonial Racial Hierarchies:**

Colonial powers often imposed racial hierarchies in their colonies, positioning white colonizers at the top and local indigenous populations at the bottom. This justified the exploitation and subjugation of colonized peoples.

Understanding these historical ideologies and pseudosciences is essential for recognizing the deep-rooted origins of racism. They highlight how racist beliefs have been constructed and used to justify discrimination, oppression, and violence. Contemporary efforts to combat racism involve challenging these historical legacies and promoting social justice and equality.

Media representation

Media representation is a critical aspect of understanding the origins and perpetuation of racism. The way racial and ethnic groups are portrayed in the media can significantly impact public perceptions and attitudes. Here are key points regarding media representation and its role in racism:

- **Stereotyping:**

Media often perpetuates racial stereotypes, portraying individuals from certain racial or ethnic backgrounds in one-dimensional and often negative ways. These stereotypes can reinforce existing prejudices and biases.

- **Underrepresentation:**

Some racial and ethnic groups are underrepresented or misrepresented in the media, leading to the erasure of their experiences and perspectives. This lack of representation can contribute to feelings of exclusion and marginalization.

- **Tokenism:**

Tokenism occurs when a few individuals from minority racial or ethnic groups are included in media but do not reflect the diversity within those groups. This token representation can create a false sense of inclusion while failing to address systemic racism.

- **Racial Profiling:**

In news reporting, racial profiling can lead to the unfair and biased coverage of criminal incidents, perpetuating stereotypes and contributing to racial prejudice.

- **Whitewashing:**

Whitewashing is the practice of casting white actors to play characters of other racial or ethnic backgrounds. This practice can erase the visibility and experiences of racial minorities in the media.

- ## **Cultural Appropriation:**

Media may perpetuate cultural appropriation by borrowing elements from other cultures without proper understanding or respect. This can reinforce stereotypes and harm cultural authenticity.

- ## **Colorism:**

Media can perpetuate colorism, favoring individuals with lighter skin tones and devaluing those with darker skin tones within racial or ethnic groups. This bias can contribute to self-esteem issues and internalized racism.

- ## **Positive Representation:**

Positive and authentic representation in media can challenge stereotypes and promote understanding. When individuals from diverse racial and ethnic backgrounds are portrayed as complex, multi-dimensional characters, it can have a significant impact on reducing prejudice.

- **Empowerment and Agency:**

Media representation that allows individuals from racial minority groups to tell their own stories and narratives can empower those communities and challenge dominant narratives.

- **Media Ownership and Control:**

The diversity of media ownership and control is critical in influencing representation. When media outlets are owned and controlled by a narrow segment of society, it can perpetuate biased narratives and exclusion.

Efforts to combat racism often involve advocating for more inclusive and equitable media representation. This includes promoting diverse voices in decision-making roles, challenging stereotypes, and supporting authentic and empowering storytelling from racial and ethnic perspectives. Recognizing the power of media to shape public attitudes is essential for addressing racism and promoting social justice.

Chapter Five: The Role of Institutions

Institutions, including governmental, educational, legal, and social organizations, play a significant role in the origins and perpetuation of racism. These institutions have the power to either reinforce or challenge systemic racism. Here are key aspects of the role of institutions in racism:

- **Government and Policy:**

Government institutions have historically enacted policies that perpetuated racial discrimination. Examples include slavery, segregation, and discriminatory voting laws. Policies that disproportionately affect racial minority groups can perpetuate disparities and reinforce racism.

- **Educational Institutions:**

Schools and educational institutions can contribute to racism through disparities in funding, resources, and disciplinary practices. Racial biases can also influence curriculum and teaching, perpetuating stereotypes and prejudice.

- **Legal System:**

The legal system can either promote or challenge racism. Racial profiling, unequal sentencing, and discriminatory practices within the criminal justice system can reinforce racial disparities. Conversely, legal measures, such as anti-discrimination laws, can help combat racism.

- **Employment and Workplaces:**

Institutions in the business and employment sector can perpetuate racism through discriminatory hiring practices, unequal pay, and limited opportunities for racial minority groups. Workplace discrimination and harassment can also create hostile environments.

- ### **Media and Entertainment:**

Media institutions, including news outlets and entertainment industries, can perpetuate stereotypes and bias. The underrepresentation or misrepresentation of racial minority groups can reinforce prejudiced attitudes.

- ### **Healthcare Institutions:**

Disparities in healthcare access and treatment can be influenced by institutional factors. Racial disparities in healthcare outcomes can be perpetuated by a lack of access to quality care and unequal treatment.

- ### **Social Services and Welfare:**

Social service institutions can inadvertently perpetuate racism through policies that disproportionately affect racial minority groups. Discriminatory practices, lack of access to resources, and systemic biases can hinder social mobility.

- ## **Housing and Real Estate:**

Housing institutions have a history of perpetuating racial discrimination through redlining, segregation, and discriminatory lending practices. These practices have led to residential disparities and limited access to safe and affordable housing.

- ## **Religious Institutions:**

Religious institutions can influence attitudes and beliefs about race. While many promote values of tolerance and inclusion, some religious organizations have contributed to discriminatory attitudes and practices.

- ## **Nonprofit and Advocacy Organizations:**

Advocacy organizations often work to challenge racism and promote social justice. They play a vital role in raising awareness, lobbying for policy changes, and offering support to affected communities.

Recognizing the role of institutions in racism is essential for understanding systemic racism. Addressing racism often involves advocating for policy changes, reforms, and shifts in institutional practices that promote equality, diversity, and inclusion. Efforts to challenge racism at the institutional level aim to create more equitable and just societies.

Government policies

Government policies have played a significant role in the origins and perpetuation of racism, as well as in efforts to combat it. The impact of government policies on racism can be profound and far-reaching. Here are some key aspects related to the role of government policies in racism:

- **Historical Racist Policies:**

Throughout history, governments have implemented and enforced policies that explicitly discriminated against racial and ethnic minority groups. Examples include slavery, segregation, forced relocation of indigenous peoples, and discriminatory immigration laws. These policies institutionalized racial inequality and oppression.

- **Jim Crow Laws:**

In the United States, Jim Crow laws were a set of state and local laws that enforced racial segregation and discrimination, particularly in the Southern states. These laws covered areas such as education, public facilities, transportation, and voting rights.

- **Redlining:**

Government policies, such as redlining, were used to segregate neighborhoods and limit access to mortgage loans and housing for racial minority groups. This practice led to disparities in housing and wealth that persist today.

- **Japanese Internment:**

During World War II, the U.S. government interned Japanese Americans in camps based solely on their Japanese ancestry. This policy is now widely recognized as a grave injustice and violation of civil rights.

- **Indian Residential Schools:**

In Canada and the United States, government policies supported Indian residential schools, where Indigenous children were forcibly separated from their families and subjected to cultural assimilation and abuse.

- **Immigration Laws:**

Immigration policies have often been influenced by racism and xenophobia. Policies like the Chinese Exclusion Act in the United States and the White Australia Policy exemplify how government policies were used to exclude or restrict immigration based on race.

- **Voting Rights:**

Historically, voting rights policies, such as literacy tests and poll taxes, were used to disenfranchise racial minority groups, particularly African Americans. The civil rights movement in the U.S. aimed to dismantle such policies.

• Affirmative Action:

In an effort to address historical discrimination, some governments have implemented affirmative action policies. These policies aim to provide opportunities and advantages to historically disadvantaged racial groups. They are often a subject of debate and controversy.

• Anti-Discrimination Laws:

Governments have also passed anti-discrimination laws to combat racism. These laws prohibit discrimination in various areas, including employment, education, housing, and public accommodations.

• Reparations:

Some governments and organizations have considered or implemented reparations policies to address the historical injustices and harms caused by racism. Reparations can take various forms, including financial compensation and community investments.

Understanding the historical and contemporary impact of government policies on racism is crucial for addressing systemic racism. Advocacy, legal reform, and public policy initiatives often play a central role in combating racism and promoting social justice. Recognizing the power of government policies to either perpetuate or challenge racism is essential for creating more equitable societies.

Educational systems

Educational systems play a significant role in shaping societal attitudes, perpetuating or challenging racism, and influencing the life trajectories of individuals from diverse racial and ethnic backgrounds. Here are key points related to the role of educational systems in racism:

- **Historical Disparities:**

Educational systems have a history of disparities in funding, resources, and opportunities based on race. This includes the segregation of schools and the provision of subpar education for racial minority groups, particularly African Americans and Indigenous peoples.

- **Curriculum and Representation:**

The curriculum and teaching materials used in schools can perpetuate racism if they lack diversity and include biased or inaccurate information. The omission of contributions and histories of racial minority groups can lead to a skewed understanding of society.

• **Bias and Discrimination:**

Discriminatory practices within educational institutions can affect racial minority students. This includes racial profiling, disciplinary disparities, and unfair treatment by educators and administrators.

• **Access to Quality Education:**

Racial disparities in educational achievement and access to quality education are common. Students from minority racial groups may attend schools with fewer resources, less experienced teachers, and inadequate facilities.

• **School-to-Prison Pipeline:**

Some educational systems contribute to the "school-to-prison pipeline," where students, primarily from racial minority backgrounds, are disproportionately disciplined and funneled into the criminal justice system rather than receiving support and guidance.

- **Affirmative Action:**

Affirmative action policies aim to address historical disparities by providing opportunities and advantages to racial minority students in higher education. These policies are often a subject of debate and legal challenges.

- **Representation and Leadership:**

The underrepresentation of racial minority teachers, administrators, and leaders in educational institutions can impact the experiences of students and the cultural competence of schools.

- **Culturally Responsive Education:**

Culturally responsive education seeks to address the needs of diverse student populations by incorporating their cultural perspectives, histories, and experiences into the curriculum and teaching methods.

- **Bilingual and Multilingual Education:**

Policies related to bilingual and multilingual education can either support the linguistic diversity of racial minority students or hinder their access to educational opportunities.

- **Diversity Training:**

Teacher training programs and professional development often include diversity and anti-bias training to help educators better understand and address the needs of students from diverse racial and ethnic backgrounds.

Educational systems have the potential to both reinforce and challenge racism. Efforts to combat racism within education include advocating for equitable funding, anti-bias training for educators, inclusive curricula, diverse representation in leadership positions, and policies that promote access to quality education for all students. Recognizing the role of educational systems in addressing racism is essential for creating more inclusive and equitable learning environments.

Legal and justice systems

Legal and justice systems play a pivotal role in addressing racism and ensuring equal treatment under the law. However, these systems have historically perpetuated racial discrimination and inequalities. Here are key points related to the role of legal and justice systems in racism:

- **Historical Discrimination:**

Legal systems have been used to enforce and legitimize racial discrimination, such as slavery, segregation, and racially biased criminal justice policies. These historical injustices continue to shape racial disparities in the present.

- **Racial Profiling:**

Racial profiling involves law enforcement or other authorities targeting individuals based on their race or ethnicity, often resulting in unwarranted scrutiny and harassment of racial minority groups.

- ## **Disparate Policing:**

Some communities, particularly racial minority communities, may experience heavier policing and harsher law enforcement tactics. This can lead to over-policing, racial bias in arrests, and racial disparities in incarceration.

- ## **Criminal Sentencing:**

Racial disparities in sentencing can be influenced by biases within the legal system. Individuals from racial minority groups may receive harsher sentences for the same offenses as white individuals.

- ## **Juvenile Justice:**

Racial disparities are often evident in the juvenile justice system, where racial minority youth are disproportionately arrested, detained, and sentenced to harsher punishments.

- ## **Bail and Pretrial Detention:**

Racial disparities exist in pretrial detention and bail decisions, where racial minority individuals are more likely to be held in custody or required to pay higher bail amounts.

- ## **Death Penalty:**

Racial bias has been a concern in death penalty cases, with racial minority defendants more likely to receive the death penalty for similar crimes as white defendants.

- ## **Exoneration:**

Racial minority individuals are overrepresented among those wrongfully convicted and later exonerated, highlighting flaws in the justice system.

- ## **Access to Legal Representation:**

Racial disparities exist in access to quality legal representation. Individuals from marginalized racial groups may have limited access to competent legal counsel, affecting the outcomes of their cases.

- **Civil Rights and Anti-Discrimination Laws:**

Legal systems have also been instrumental in promoting equality and justice. Civil rights and anti-discrimination laws, such as the Civil Rights Act, the Voting Rights Act, and the Fair Housing Act in the United States, have been critical in challenging racism and racial discrimination.

Efforts to combat racism within legal and justice systems involve reforms in policing, sentencing, and criminal justice procedures. Promoting diversity within the legal profession and increasing transparency and accountability in law enforcement are also crucial steps. Legal and justice systems have the potential to be powerful tools in the fight against racism, but ongoing vigilance and reform are needed to ensure that they uphold the principles of justice and equality for all.

Chapter Six: Resistance and Movements

Resistance and movements have been central to combating racism and advocating for social justice. Throughout history, individuals and communities have organized and mobilized to challenge racial discrimination and inequality. Here are key aspects of resistance and movements in the fight against racism:

- **Civil Rights Movement:**

The Civil Rights Movement in the United States, primarily in the 1950s and 1960s, was a watershed moment in the fight against racial segregation, discrimination, and voting restrictions. It led to the passage of significant civil rights legislation, including the Civil Rights Act of 1964 and the Voting Rights Act of 1965.

- ## Anti-Apartheid Movement:

The anti-apartheid movement in South Africa and internationally aimed to end the apartheid system, which institutionalized racial segregation and discrimination. This movement played a pivotal role in dismantling apartheid and promoting racial equality.

- ## Black Lives Matter (BLM):

The BLM movement, which emerged in the United States in 2013, focuses on addressing racial profiling, police brutality, and systemic racism. It has sparked global protests and raised awareness about the disproportionate impact of racism on Black communities.

- ## Indigenous Rights Movements:

Indigenous peoples around the world have organized movements to advocate for their rights, land, and self-determination. These movements challenge the historical and ongoing colonization and dispossession of Indigenous communities.

• **Afrofuturism:**

Afrofuturism is a cultural and artistic movement that explores themes of Black empowerment, resistance, and liberation through science fiction, art, and literature.

• **Asian American Activism:**

Asian American activists have advocated for civil rights and social justice, including the fight against discriminatory immigration policies, racial profiling, and violence against Asian communities.

• **Latino and Chicano Movements:**

Movements such as the Chicano Movement and the United Farm Workers' movement have sought to address issues like labor rights, education, and political representation for Latino and Chicano communities.

• **Intersectional Movements:**

Many contemporary movements recognize the interconnectedness of various forms of discrimination and injustice, including racism, sexism, homophobia, and more. Intersectional movements seek to address these intersecting oppressions.

• **Online Activism:**

Social media and online platforms have become powerful tools for raising awareness, organizing protests, and advocating for racial justice. Hashtags like #SayHerName and #StopAsianHate have gained traction in addressing racial issues.

• **Decolonization Movements:**

Movements for decolonization seek to address the historical legacies of colonialism, often by advocating for Indigenous rights, land restitution, and the reclamation of cultural heritage.

Resistance and movements are essential in challenging racism, raising awareness, and pressuring governments and institutions to address systemic discrimination. They reflect the collective efforts of individuals and communities to create more equitable and inclusive societies. These movements have led to important social and policy changes, but the struggle for racial justice continues in many parts of the world.

Civil rights movements

Civil rights movements have been pivotal in addressing racial discrimination, segregation, and inequalities, particularly in the United States. These movements have had a profound impact on advancing civil rights and social justice. Here are some of the most significant civil rights movements:

- **African American Civil Rights Movement:**

The African American Civil Rights Movement, often associated with the 1950s and 1960s, sought to end racial segregation and discrimination. Key events include the Montgomery Bus Boycott, the March on Washington for Jobs and Freedom, and the Civil Rights Act of 1964.

- **Women's Rights Movement:**

The Women's Rights Movement has intersected with civil rights efforts, advocating for gender equality and the rights of women. Figures like Rosa Parks and Ella Baker were instrumental in both movements.

- **Native American Civil Rights Movement:**

Indigenous activists and movements have fought for the recognition of Indigenous sovereignty, land rights, and cultural preservation. The American Indian Movement (AIM) is a notable example.

- **Latino Civil Rights Movement:**

Movements such as the United Farm Workers, led by Cesar Chavez and Dolores Huerta, advocated for the rights of Latino farmworkers and laborers. Additionally, the Chicano Movement sought political empowerment and educational equity.

- **LGBTQ+ Civil Rights Movement:**

This movement has advocated for LGBTQ+ rights, including the decriminalization of homosexuality, anti-discrimination laws, and the fight for marriage equality. The Stonewall riots of 1969 marked a significant moment in this movement.

- **Disability Rights Movement:**

Advocates for disability rights have pushed for equal access to public spaces, employment, and educational opportunities. The Americans with Disabilities Act (ADA) was a landmark achievement in this movement.

- **Asian American Civil Rights Movement:**

Asian American activists have worked to challenge discriminatory immigration policies, promote civil rights, and address issues such as racial profiling and discrimination.

- ## Human Rights Movement:

The broader human rights movement has aimed to address global injustices, including those related to racial discrimination, apartheid, and colonialism. The fight against apartheid in South Africa is one prominent example.

- ## Modern Civil Rights Movement:

Contemporary civil rights movements, such as Black Lives Matter (BLM), continue to advocate for racial justice, police reform, and an end to systemic racism, particularly in the United States.

- ## Intersectional Movements:

Many contemporary movements recognize the interconnected nature of various forms of discrimination and advocate for racial and social justice using an intersectional lens.

These civil rights movements have played a crucial role in challenging and dismantling systemic racism, advocating for equal rights, and raising awareness about the impact of discrimination on marginalized communities. While significant progress has been made, the fight for civil rights and racial justice continues in many parts of the world, emphasizing the need for ongoing advocacy and change.

Anti-racism activism

Anti-racism activism is a vital and ongoing effort to challenge and eradicate racism in all its forms. It encompasses a range of actions and strategies aimed at promoting equality, justice, and social change. Here are key components of anti-racism activism:

- **Awareness and Education:**

Anti-racism activism begins with self-education and awareness. Activists often engage in reading, research, and dialogue to deepen their understanding of racism and its manifestations.

- **Challenging Bias:**

Anti-racism activists confront their own biases and prejudices and actively work to challenge and unlearn them. This process involves self-reflection and personal growth.

- ## **Advocacy and Allyship:**

Activists advocate for racial justice by standing in solidarity with marginalized racial and ethnic groups. Allies use their privilege to support those facing discrimination and to amplify their voices.

- ## **Protests and Demonstrations:**

Participating in peaceful protests and demonstrations is a powerful way to raise awareness of racial injustices and call for change. Movements like Black Lives Matter have organized mass protests against police brutality and systemic racism.

- ## **Community Organizing:**

Activists often engage in grassroots community organizing to address specific racial injustices and systemic issues. This can include forming advocacy groups, community forums, and local initiatives.

- **Legislative and Policy Advocacy:**

Advocacy for policy changes and legislative reform is a key aspect of anti-racism activism. Activists lobby for laws and policies that promote racial equality and challenge those that perpetuate discrimination.

- **Supporting Racially Marginalized Communities:**

Anti-racism activists work to support and uplift marginalized communities through donations, volunteering, and initiatives that address their unique needs.

- **Raising Awareness:**

Spreading awareness about racial injustices through social media, writing, art, and other forms of communication is an essential part of anti-racism work.

- **Educational Initiatives:**

Activists may work within educational institutions to promote anti-racist curricula, diversity training, and inclusive practices.

- **Economic Activism:**

Economic activism includes initiatives like supporting businesses owned by racial minorities and advocating for equitable hiring and promotion practices within corporations.

- **Art and Culture:**

Activists may use art, literature, and cultural expressions to challenge stereotypes, highlight racial injustices, and promote empathy and understanding.

- **Legal Action:**

Legal organizations and activists use the legal system to challenge racial discrimination, file lawsuits, and seek justice for victims of racism.

- **International Solidarity:**

Anti-racism activism often extends beyond national borders, as activists collaborate on global issues related to racism, colonialism, and racial justice.

Anti-racism activism is a multi-faceted and ongoing commitment to challenging systemic racism and promoting a more equitable and inclusive society. It involves the collective efforts of individuals, organizations, and communities to address the root causes of racial discrimination and inequality.

Progress and challenges

Progress and challenges are intertwined in the ongoing struggle to combat racism and promote racial equity. While significant strides have been made, racism persists in various forms, and addressing it remains a complex and evolving endeavor. Here are some aspects of progress and challenges in the fight against racism:

Progress:

- **Legal Advances:**

Legal changes and anti-discrimination laws have been enacted in many countries, providing a framework for addressing racial disparities and discrimination.

- **Awareness and Education:**

There is increased awareness about racism and its impact, facilitated by educational initiatives, social media, and public discourse.

- **Social Movements:**

The emergence of social movements like Black Lives Matter has raised awareness and mobilized individuals to demand change.

- **Representation:**

There is growing recognition of the importance of diverse representation in media, politics, and corporate leadership.

- **Policy Reforms:**

Reforms in policing, criminal justice, and other sectors are being pursued in response to calls for change.

- **Diversity Initiatives:**

Organizations and institutions are implementing diversity and inclusion programs to address racial disparities.

Challenges:

- **Systemic Racism:**

Systemic racism remains deeply embedded in many institutions and societal structures, making it challenging to dismantle.

- **Implicit Bias:**

Implicit bias, which affects individuals' attitudes and behaviors unconsciously, continues to contribute to racial disparities.

- **White Supremacy:**

White supremacy and extremist ideologies persist and can fuel acts of racial violence.

- **Economic Disparities:**

Racial disparities in income, wealth, and employment remain significant, perpetuating inequality.

- **Healthcare Disparities:**

Racial disparities in healthcare outcomes have been highlighted, especially in the context of the COVID-19 pandemic.

- **Educational Inequities:**

Educational systems often perpetuate racial disparities, with inadequate resources and opportunities for racial minority students.

- **Hate Crimes and Discrimination:**

Hate crimes, discrimination, and racial violence continue to pose significant challenges to racial minority communities.

- **Resistance to Change:**

Some segments of society may resist efforts to address racial inequality and systemic racism, viewing these efforts as threats to the status quo.

- **Intersectionality:**

The intersection of race with other forms of discrimination (e.g., gender, sexual orientation) presents complex challenges in addressing multiple layers of identity-based discrimination.

- **Global Inequities:**

Racial inequalities and injustices are not limited to one region or country; they are global issues requiring international collaboration and advocacy.

Progress in combating racism requires ongoing commitment and action. It involves addressing not only overt forms of discrimination but also the root causes and systemic structures that perpetuate racial disparities. Challenges are significant, but they serve as a reminder of the work that remains to be done and the importance of collective efforts to create a more equitable and just society.

Chapter Seven: Contemporary Issues

Contemporary issues related to racism encompass a wide range of challenges and debates that continue to shape society. These issues highlight the ongoing need to address racial discrimination and promote racial equity. Some of the key contemporary issues related to racism include:

- **Police Brutality and Racial Profiling:**

Incidents of police brutality and racial profiling disproportionately affect racial minority communities. Protests and movements like Black Lives Matter have drawn attention to these issues and called for police reform.

- **Voting Rights:**

Efforts to restrict voting access, particularly for racial minority groups, are a pressing concern. Advocates are working to protect and expand voting rights.

• Hate Crimes and Discrimination:

Hate crimes against racial minority groups, as well as discrimination in employment, housing, and other areas, persist as significant issues.

• Education Inequities:

Educational systems continue to show racial disparities in funding, resources, disciplinary practices, and achievement.

• Healthcare Disparities:

Racial disparities in healthcare access and outcomes have been highlighted by the COVID-19 pandemic, drawing attention to inequities in health systems.

- **Economic Inequality:**

Racial disparities in income, wealth, and employment opportunities persist and are exacerbated by systemic factors.

- **Mass Incarceration:**

The overrepresentation of racial minority groups in the criminal justice system and issues of racial bias in sentencing continue to be a concern.

- **Immigration Policy:**

Discriminatory immigration policies, deportations, and detention centers disproportionately affect immigrants from racial minority backgrounds.

- **Cultural Appropriation:**

The appropriation of elements from other cultures without proper understanding or respect remains a contentious issue, perpetuating racial insensitivity.

- **Anti-Asian Hate:**

A rise in anti-Asian hate crimes and discrimination has been observed, fueled in part by the COVID-19 pandemic and xenophobia.

- **Microaggressions and Implicit Bias:**

Microaggressions and implicit bias continue to harm racial minority individuals, affecting daily interactions and experiences.

- **Climate Justice:**

The impact of climate change disproportionately affects vulnerable communities, including many racial minority groups.

- **International Racism:**

Racism and xenophobia are not confined to one country; global events and issues, such as refugee crises, have international implications.

- **Racial Equity in Technology:**

The tech industry faces concerns regarding diversity, inclusion, and bias in artificial intelligence and algorithms, which can perpetuate racial disparities.

- **Environmental Racism:**

Communities of color often bear the brunt of environmental hazards and pollution due to discriminatory land-use policies.

- **LGBTQ+ Discrimination:**

Racial minority members of the LGBTQ+ community can face intersecting forms of discrimination and violence.

Contemporary issues related to racism underscore the importance of addressing the systemic and structural aspects of racial discrimination. Anti-racist efforts aim to create a more inclusive and equitable society, and these ongoing challenges highlight the need for collective action, advocacy, and policy changes to effect positive change.

Ongoing racial disparities

Ongoing racial disparities continue to persist in various aspects of society, reflecting the deep-rooted effects of historical racism and systemic inequities. These disparities are evident in areas such as:

- **Economic Disparities:**

Racial minority groups, particularly Black and Hispanic communities, face significant economic disparities. They often have lower incomes, higher unemployment rates, and limited access to wealth-building opportunities, such as homeownership and investments.

- **Education:**

Racial disparities in education persist, including unequal access to quality schools, lower high school graduation rates, and limited representation in higher education institutions.

- ## **Criminal Justice:**

Racial minority individuals, especially Black Americans, are disproportionately represented in the criminal justice system. They face higher rates of arrest, longer sentences, and are more likely to be victims of police violence.

- ## **Healthcare:**

Racial disparities in healthcare outcomes and access to healthcare persist. These disparities have been exacerbated by the COVID-19 pandemic, with racial minority communities experiencing higher infection and mortality rates.

- ## **Housing:**

Racial minorities often face housing discrimination, limited access to affordable housing, and the effects of redlining and housing segregation policies from the past.

- **Voting Rights:**

Efforts to restrict voting access, particularly in minority communities, undermine the principles of democracy and disproportionately affect racial minority voters.

- **Employment:**

Racial minority groups are more likely to experience employment discrimination, wage gaps, and underrepresentation in higher-paying and leadership positions.

- **Wealth Gap:**

The wealth gap between racial minority groups and white Americans is significant and has far-reaching effects on economic stability and intergenerational wealth transfer.

- **Climate Justice:**

Communities of color often bear the brunt of environmental hazards and pollution due to discriminatory land-use policies, affecting their health and quality of life.

- **Cultural and Media Representation:**

Racial minorities are often underrepresented or misrepresented in the media, leading to limited visibility and perpetuating stereotypes.

- **Education Funding:**

Schools in predominantly racial minority neighborhoods often receive less funding and fewer resources, resulting in educational disparities.

- **Discrimination and Microaggressions:**

Racial minorities continue to face discrimination, microaggressions, and racial bias in daily interactions, which can negatively impact their mental and emotional well-being.

- **Mental Health Disparities:**

Racial minorities often have limited access to mental health services and face disparities in mental health outcomes.

- **Criminalization of Communities:**

Some communities of color are disproportionately criminalized, leading to harsher penalties and higher rates of incarceration.

These ongoing racial disparities highlight the need for continued efforts to address systemic racism, promote racial equity, and dismantle the structural barriers that perpetuate inequality. Advocacy, policy reforms, community organizing, and public awareness are essential tools in combating these disparities and creating a more just and inclusive society.

Intersectionality

Intersectionality is a concept that recognizes the interconnected nature of social categories and identities, such as race, gender, class, sexuality, and more. It was coined by legal scholar Kimberlé Crenshaw in the late 1980s and has since become a foundational framework for understanding how multiple forms of discrimination and privilege intersect and interact. Here are key points about intersectionality:

- **Intersecting Identities:**

Intersectionality emphasizes that individuals hold multiple social identities simultaneously, and these identities can intersect in complex ways. For example, a person can be both a woman and a racial minority, and these aspects of their identity can intersect to create unique experiences and challenges.

- **Social Inequalities:**

Intersectionality recognizes that social inequalities are not additive; they are interconnected and can compound one another. A person's experience of discrimination is influenced by the interplay of multiple identities and forms of privilege.

- **Understanding Systems of Oppression:**

Intersectionality provides a framework for understanding how systems of oppression, such as racism, sexism, homophobia, and classism, interact and reinforce one another. It highlights the need to address the interconnected systems of discrimination.

- **Complexity of Identity:**

Each individual's identity is complex, shaped by their race, gender, sexuality, socioeconomic status, disability, and more. Intersectionality recognizes the richness and complexity of human identity.

- **Inclusivity and Solidarity:**

Intersectionality promotes inclusivity and solidarity. It encourages individuals to recognize and support those whose experiences differ due to their intersecting identities.

- **Policy and Activism:**

Intersectionality has implications for policy and activism. It calls for policies and movements that address the specific needs of people with multiple marginalized identities.

- **Critique of Mainstream Feminism:**

Intersectionality has been used to critique mainstream feminism for its historical focus on the experiences of white, middle-class women. It emphasizes the need for a more inclusive and diverse feminist movement.

- **Legal and Social Justice:**

In legal contexts, intersectionality is used to advocate for rights and protections for individuals who face discrimination based on multiple aspects of their identity.

Intersectionality is a powerful framework for understanding and addressing the complexities of discrimination and privilege. It highlights the importance of recognizing the unique experiences of individuals with intersecting identities and underscores the need for a more inclusive and equitable approach to social justice and activism.

Global perspectives on racism

Racism is a global issue that transcends national boundaries and affects people from diverse racial and ethnic backgrounds around the world. Different countries and regions have their own unique experiences with racism, but there are common global perspectives on this issue:

- **Historical Context:**

The history of colonialism, imperialism, and slavery has left a lasting legacy of racial discrimination and inequality in many parts of the world. Historical injustices continue to shape the experiences of racial minority groups today.

- **Systemic Racism:**

Systemic racism is not limited to a specific country. It is a global phenomenon that manifests in various forms, including discriminatory policies, practices, and institutional biases.

- **International Human Rights:**

International human rights organizations, such as the United Nations, have recognized racism as a violation of human rights. Global conventions, like the International Convention on the Elimination of All Forms of Racial Discrimination, seek to combat racial discrimination on a worldwide scale.

- **Xenophobia and Discrimination:**

Racial discrimination is closely tied to xenophobia and discrimination against migrants and refugees. This issue has been exacerbated by global migration patterns and refugee crises.

- **Intersectionality:**

The concept of intersectionality is applicable worldwide, as individuals often face multiple forms of discrimination based on their race, gender, class, and other identities.

- **Global Movements:**

Movements like Black Lives Matter and the fight against apartheid in South Africa have had international implications, raising awareness of racial injustices and inspiring global solidarity.

- **Cultural Stereotypes:**

Cultural stereotypes and misrepresentations in media are not confined to one country. They perpetuate bias and misunderstanding on a global scale.

- **Climate Justice:**

Climate change disproportionately affects vulnerable communities, including many racial minority groups. The global environmental justice movement recognizes this intersection of environmental and racial issues.

- **Refugee and Asylum Seeker Rights:**

Discrimination and racial profiling of refugees and asylum seekers occur in various regions, highlighting the need for global advocacy and support for those fleeing persecution.

- **International Solidarity:**

Activists and organizations work to build international solidarity in the fight against racism and colonial legacies.

- **Global Anti-Racism Efforts:**

Worldwide, there are efforts to address racism through education, awareness campaigns, policy changes, and advocacy. Many countries have established national institutions and mechanisms to combat racial discrimination.

• **Challenges and Progress:**

Different regions face unique challenges and make varying degrees of progress in addressing racism. Sharing lessons and strategies can be beneficial for the global movement against racial discrimination.

Recognizing racism as a global issue is essential for fostering international cooperation, addressing root causes, and advocating for racial justice on a global scale. While specific contexts and experiences vary, the fight against racism is a collective effort that transcends borders and unites people in their commitment to equality and social justice.

Chapter Eight: Future Prospects

The future prospects in the fight against racism are both hopeful and challenging. While significant progress has been made, there is still work to be done to address systemic racism and promote racial equity. Here are some future prospects and considerations:

- **Continued Activism:**

Ongoing activism and advocacy will play a vital role in challenging racism. Movements like Black Lives Matter and global anti-racism efforts are likely to continue their work to raise awareness and demand change.

- **Policy Reforms:**

The push for policy reforms, particularly in areas like criminal justice, education, and voting rights, will continue. Changes in legislation are critical for dismantling systemic racism.

- **Education and Awareness:**

Educational initiatives and awareness campaigns will help individuals understand and confront racism, bias, and privilege.

- **Institutional Change:**

Organizations and institutions are increasingly recognizing the importance of diversity, equity, and inclusion. This trend is likely to continue, with more institutions adopting anti-racist policies and practices.

- **Intersecting Movements:**

Intersectionality and the recognition of intersecting forms of discrimination will become more integrated into activism and policy efforts.

- **Youth Engagement:**

Young people are often at the forefront of social justice movements. Their involvement and activism will shape the future of anti-racism efforts.

- **Global Collaboration:**

International collaboration and solidarity will strengthen the fight against racism on a global scale. Sharing strategies and insights across borders will be crucial.

- **Media Representation:**

Increased representation and more accurate portrayals of racial minority groups in media and entertainment will contribute to greater understanding and empathy.

- **Mental Health Support:**

Efforts to address the mental health impact of racism and discrimination will expand, providing support for affected individuals.

- **Environmental Justice:**

The intersection of environmental and racial issues will gain more attention, as communities of color are disproportionately affected by environmental hazards.

- **Anti-Racist Education:**

Anti-racist education will become more prevalent in schools and institutions, helping future generations better understand and combat racism.

Challenges to Address:

- **Deep-Rooted Systemic Racism:**

Systemic racism is deeply ingrained in many institutions and structures. Overcoming this will require sustained effort and vigilance.

- **Resistance to Change:**

There will be resistance to efforts aimed at dismantling racism, as some individuals and groups may perceive these changes as threats to the status quo.

- **Xenophobia and Nationalism:**

Rising nationalism and xenophobia in some parts of the world can hinder international collaboration and efforts to address global racism.

- **Economic Disparities:**

Addressing economic disparities, particularly the wealth gap, is a complex and long-term challenge.

- **Political Polarization:**

Political polarization can impede progress in addressing racial discrimination, as issues related to racism often become politicized.

The future prospects for addressing racism are hopeful, as there is a growing awareness and commitment to combat discrimination. However, these efforts will require ongoing dedication, policy changes, and international collaboration to achieve lasting racial equity and social justice.

The path to a more equitable society

The path to a more equitable society, one that truly values diversity and ensures justice for all, is a complex and ongoing journey. It involves multiple facets and requires collective effort. Here are key steps and considerations along this path:

- **Education and Awareness:**

Promote anti-racist education and awareness programs in schools, workplaces, and communities. These initiatives should teach the history of racial injustice and the importance of empathy and allyship.

- **Policy and Legislative Changes:**

Advocate for policy reforms at local, national, and international levels. This includes changes in criminal justice, voting rights, housing, education, and economic policies that address systemic racism.

- **Economic Equity:**

Address economic disparities by implementing policies that promote economic equity, affordable housing, access to quality jobs, and wealth-building opportunities for racial minority communities.

- **Diversity and Inclusion:**

Encourage diversity and inclusion in all sectors, including government, business, academia, and the arts. This involves diversity in leadership, equitable hiring practices, and creating inclusive work and educational environments.

- **Accountability and Transparency:**

Hold institutions, corporations, and governments accountable for discriminatory practices and policies. Promote transparency in data reporting and decision-making processes.

- ## Community Building:

Foster community engagement and support networks that empower marginalized communities. This includes providing access to healthcare, mental health services, and social services.

- ## Restorative Justice:

Embrace restorative justice practices to address the harms caused by racial discrimination and violence, both historically and in the present.

- ## Cultural Representation:

Promote accurate and respectful representation of racial minority groups in media, art, and cultural institutions. Challenge stereotypes and misrepresentations.

- ## Environmental Justice:

Address environmental racism by acknowledging the disproportionate impact of pollution and environmental hazards on marginalized communities. Advocate for clean and safe environments for all.

- **Global Collaboration:**

Recognize that racism is a global issue, and collaborate internationally to combat it. Share strategies, support global anti-racism efforts, and work together to dismantle the systems that perpetuate discrimination.

- **Intersectionality:**

Recognize the intersection of racial discrimination with other forms of oppression, such as gender, sexual orientation, and class. Develop inclusive policies and initiatives that account for these intersections.

- **Youth Engagement:**

Encourage young people to become active agents of change. Their involvement in activism and advocacy is vital for shaping a more equitable future.

- **Mental Health Support:**

Provide accessible mental health services and support for individuals who have been affected by racism and discrimination.

- **Civil Engagement:**

Encourage civic engagement, voting, and political participation as mechanisms for promoting change and holding elected officials accountable.

- **Resistance to Racism:**

Actively challenge racism and discrimination in your own life. Speak up against racial bias and discrimination when you encounter it.

The path to a more equitable society requires long-term commitment and an understanding of the interconnected nature of social justice issues. It's about dismantling systems of oppression and creating a world where all individuals have equal access to opportunities and are treated with respect and dignity, regardless of their race or ethnicity.

Strategies for combating racism

Combatting racism requires a multifaceted approach that addresses the root causes, promotes awareness, and actively works to dismantle discriminatory systems. Here are strategies for combating racism:

- **Education and Awareness:**

Promote anti-racist education in schools, workplaces, and communities.

Encourage open and honest conversations about racism and its impact.

Learn about the history of racial injustice and its ongoing effects.

Promote Diversity and Inclusion:

Embrace diversity and inclusion in all sectors, from business and government to academia and the arts.

Implement equitable hiring practices and promote diverse leadership.

Policy Reforms:

Advocate for policy changes at local, national, and international levels to address systemic racism.

Support criminal justice reform, voting rights protection, and equitable economic policies.

Accountability:

Hold institutions, corporations, and governments accountable for discriminatory practices.

Encourage transparency in data reporting and decision-making processes.

Community Building:

Foster community engagement and support networks that empower marginalized communities.

Ensure access to quality healthcare, mental health services, and social services.

Restorative Justice:

Embrace restorative justice practices to address the harms caused by racial discrimination and violence.

Seek reconciliation and healing through community dialogue.

Cultural Representation:

Promote accurate and respectful representation of racial minority groups in media, art, and cultural institutions.

Challenge stereotypes and misrepresentations.

Environmental Justice:

Address environmental racism by recognizing the disproportionate impact of pollution and environmental hazards on marginalized communities.

Advocate for clean and safe environments for all.

Global Collaboration:

Recognize that racism is a global issue and collaborate internationally to combat it.

Share strategies and support global anti-racism efforts.

Intersectionality:

Recognize the intersection of racial discrimination with other forms of oppression, such as gender, sexual orientation, and class.

Develop inclusive policies and initiatives that account for these intersections.

Youth Engagement:

Encourage young people to become active agents of change through activism and advocacy.

Support their involvement in social justice movements.

Mental Health Support:

Provide accessible mental health services and support for individuals affected by racism and discrimination.

Address the mental health impact of racial injustices.

Civil Engagement:

Encourage civic engagement, voting, and political participation as mechanisms for promoting change and holding elected officials accountable.

Resistance to Racism:

Actively challenge racism and discrimination in your own life.

Speak up against racial bias and discrimination when you encounter it.

Allyship:

Be an ally to racial minority communities by supporting their causes and advocating for their rights.

Listen and learn from their experiences.

Economic Equity:

Advocate for policies and initiatives that promote economic equity, affordable housing, and access to quality jobs for racial minority communities.

Media Literacy:

Develop media literacy skills to critically assess and challenge biased and harmful representations in media and online.

Economic Support:

Support businesses owned by racial minorities and invest in communities that have been historically marginalized.

Combating racism is a long-term commitment that requires collective action, empathy, and an understanding of the complex and interconnected nature of racial discrimination. These strategies, when implemented collectively, can contribute to positive change and the dismantling of discriminatory systems.

Hope for a better future

There is hope for a better future in the ongoing fight against racism. While the challenges are significant, the collective efforts of individuals, communities, and organizations are driving positive change. Here's why there is hope for a more equitable and just future:

- **Social Movements:**

The emergence of powerful social movements, such as Black Lives Matter, has raised awareness and mobilized people to demand change and challenge systemic racism.

- **Youth Activism:**

Young people are actively engaged in advocating for racial justice, demonstrating a strong commitment to creating a more inclusive future.

• Global Solidarity:

The fight against racism is a global effort. International collaboration and solidarity are fostering a sense of unity in addressing this issue.

• Policy Reforms:

Advocacy efforts have led to policy reforms at local, national, and international levels. These changes are helping to dismantle discriminatory systems and address racial inequalities.

• Cultural Shifts:

There is a growing cultural shift towards greater understanding, empathy, and inclusivity. More individuals and organizations are recognizing the importance of diversity and inclusion.

• Educational Initiatives:

Anti-racist education is becoming more prevalent in schools and institutions, empowering future generations with the knowledge and tools to challenge racism.

- **Corporate Responsibility:**

Many corporations are acknowledging their role in addressing racial disparities and are implementing diversity and inclusion initiatives.

- **Community Empowerment:**

Communities, especially those historically marginalized, are building their strength and resilience through grassroots efforts and mutual support networks.

- **Media Representation:**

Efforts to promote accurate and respectful representation of racial minority groups in media and cultural institutions are making an impact.

- **Mental Health Support:**

Increased awareness of the mental health impact of racism is leading to better support and resources for affected individuals.

- **Environmental Justice:**

The intersection of environmental and racial issues is gaining attention, with more efforts to protect vulnerable communities from environmental hazards.

- **Restorative Justice:**

Practices like restorative justice are facilitating reconciliation and healing in communities affected by racial discrimination.

- **Youth Empowerment:**

Young people are becoming agents of change, advocating for their rights and demanding a more equitable and just future.

- **Global Collaboration:**

Collaboration on a global scale is expanding the reach and impact of anti-racism efforts.

While the journey to a more equitable and just future is ongoing, the collective commitment to challenging racism and dismantling discriminatory systems is a powerful force for positive change. With continued dedication and solidarity, there is indeed hope for a better and more inclusive world.

Chapter Nine: Conclusion

In conclusion, the fight against racism is an ongoing, multifaceted, and collective endeavor that spans history and geography. It is a struggle rooted in addressing systemic discrimination and promoting racial equity. The understanding of the origins of racism, the importance of acknowledging its historical context, and the comprehensive exploration of factors contributing to racial disparities all play a crucial role in shaping the path forward.

The awareness of the ongoing racial disparities, the significance of intersectionality, and the global perspective on racism emphasize the complexity and interconnected nature of the issue. Progress and challenges coexist on this journey, reminding us of the work that remains to be done.

Strategies for combating racism offer actionable steps, from education and policy reforms to community building and economic equity. The hope for a better future lies in the collective efforts to dismantle discriminatory systems, challenge stereotypes, and foster inclusivity, empathy, and justice.

In the face of the challenges, there is reason for hope. Social movements, youth activism, global solidarity, policy reforms, and cultural shifts are indicative of the positive changes already underway. The path to a more equitable society is illuminated by the commitment of individuals, communities, and organizations, as well as the understanding that the fight against racism is a shared responsibility.

As we move forward, it is with the belief that the pursuit of racial justice is a moral imperative, and the realization that it requires long-term dedication, empathy, and a commitment to fostering a world where all individuals are treated with respect, dignity, and equity, regardless of their race or ethnicity.

Recap of key points

Certainly, here is a recap of the key points discussed in our conversation on the origin of racism, its impact, and strategies to combat it:

- **Definition of Racism:**

Racism is a belief system and set of practices that discriminate against individuals or groups based on their race or ethnicity.

- **Importance of Understanding Its Origins:**

Understanding the historical, cultural, and systemic origins of racism is essential to address its impact and dismantle discriminatory systems.

- **Overview of the Book's Approach:**

The book explores the origins of racism by examining historical context, early human societies, exploration and colonialism, the transatlantic slave trade, biological and psychological factors, evolutionary perspectives, cognitive biases, social identity theory, socioeconomic factors, economic disparities, social hierarchies, power structures, cultural and ideological factors, cultural stereotypes, historical ideologies and pseudosciences, media representation, the role of institutions, government policies, educational systems, legal and justice systems, resistance and movements, civil rights movements, and anti-racism activism.

- **Historical Context:**

Historical events, such as colonialism and slavery, have played a significant role in shaping racial discrimination and systemic racism.

- **Early Human Societies:**

Early human societies had diverse ways of organizing and categorizing people based on characteristics like race, but these did not necessarily lead to modern racism.

- **Exploration and Colonialism:**

Exploration and colonialism were pivotal in spreading and institutionalizing racial discrimination, as they involved the subjugation and exploitation of indigenous peoples.

- **Transatlantic Slave Trade:**

The transatlantic slave trade was a tragic chapter in history, resulting in the forced enslavement and racial dehumanization of African peoples.

- **Biological and Psychological Factors:**

Biological theories and psychological biases have contributed to the perpetuation of racist ideas and practices.

- **Evolutionary Perspectives:**

Some evolutionary theories have been misused to justify racist beliefs, though they do not inherently support such ideas.

- **Cognitive Biases and Prejudice:**

Cognitive biases, including implicit bias, can lead to racial prejudice and discrimination.

- **Social Identity Theory:**

Social identity theory explains how people form identities based on group memberships and can lead to in-group favoritism and out-group bias.

- **Socioeconomic Factors:**

Socioeconomic disparities play a role in perpetuating racial inequalities in income, employment, education, and housing.

- **Economic Disparities:**

Racial disparities in wealth and income continue to be a major issue, with far-reaching effects on financial stability and opportunity.

- **Social Hierarchies and Classism:**

Social hierarchies often intersect with race, leading to discrimination and inequality based on both race and socioeconomic status.

- **Power Structures:**

Power structures and institutions can reinforce racial discrimination and are essential to address in the fight against racism.

- **Cultural and Ideological Factors:**

Cultural beliefs and ideologies have historically played a role in shaping racist attitudes and practices.

- **Cultural Stereotypes:**

Cultural stereotypes perpetuate bias and misunderstanding, contributing to racial discrimination.

- **Historical Ideologies and Pseudosciences:**

Historical ideologies and pseudosciences have been used to justify racism and discriminatory policies.

- **Media Representation:**

Accurate and respectful media representation of racial minority groups is essential to challenge stereotypes and bias.

- **The Role of Institutions:**

Institutions, including government, education, and justice systems, are responsible for perpetuating or challenging racial discrimination.

- **Government Policies:**

Government policies have historically contributed to racial discrimination, but they also have the power to enact reforms and promote equality.

- **Educational Systems:**

Educational systems can perpetuate racial disparities and inequality, but they are also a key avenue for change through anti-racist education and policies.

- **Legal and Justice Systems:**

Legal and justice systems have historically been involved in racial discrimination, but they can also be instruments of justice and equality.

- **Resistance and Movements:**

Resistance and movements, such as civil rights and anti-racism activism, are essential in challenging systemic racism and advocating for change.

- **Civil Rights Movements:**

Civil rights movements have historically played a crucial role in advancing racial equality and challenging discriminatory laws and practices.

- **Anti-Racism Activism:**

Anti-racism activism involves a range of actions and strategies aimed at promoting equality, justice, and social change.

- **Progress and Challenges:**

Progress has been made in the fight against racism, but challenges persist, including systemic racism, implicit bias, and resistance to change.

- **Contemporary Issues:**

Contemporary issues related to racism include police brutality, voting rights, hate crimes, discrimination, healthcare disparities, educational inequities, economic disparities, mass incarceration, and environmental racism.

- **Ongoing Racial Disparities:**

Racial disparities continue in various aspects of society, including economics, education, criminal justice, healthcare, and voting rights.

- **Intersectionality:**

Intersectionality recognizes the interconnected nature of social identities and how they can compound discrimination and privilege.

- **Global Perspectives on Racism:**

Racism is a global issue, with shared experiences and challenges, and it requires international collaboration and solidarity.

- **Hope for a Better Future:**

There is hope for a better future in the fight against racism, as movements, youth activism, policy reforms, and global collaboration are driving positive change.

- **Strategies for Combating Racism:**

Strategies for combating racism include education and awareness, policy reforms, accountability, diversity and inclusion, community building,

Call to action

The fight against racism is a shared responsibility that requires ongoing commitment and collective action. Here is a call to action for individuals, communities, and organizations:

- **Educate Yourself:**

Take the time to learn about the history of racism, its origins, and its ongoing impact. Reading books, watching documentaries, and engaging in anti-racist education can provide essential knowledge.

- **Listen and Learn:**

Listen to the experiences and perspectives of racial minority individuals. Engage in open and empathetic conversations to better understand their lived experiences.

- **Challenge Bias:**

Actively challenge racial bias and discrimination in your own life and in your interactions with others. Speak up against racism when you encounter it.

- **Promote Anti-Racist Education:**

Advocate for anti-racist education in schools and institutions. Support curricula that teach the history of racial injustice and the importance of empathy.

- **Support Policy Reforms:**

Advocate for policy changes at the local, national, and international levels. These policies should address systemic racism and promote racial equity.

- **Promote Diversity and Inclusion:**

Encourage diversity and inclusion in workplaces, government, academia, and the arts. Support equitable hiring practices and diverse leadership.

- **Hold Institutions Accountable:**

Hold institutions, corporations, and governments accountable for discriminatory practices. Demand transparency in data reporting and decision-making processes.

- **Support Community Empowerment:**

Support community-building efforts that empower marginalized communities. Ensure access to quality healthcare, mental health services, and social services.

- **Promote Accurate Representation:**

Advocate for accurate and respectful representation of racial minority groups in media, art, and cultural institutions. Challenge stereotypes and misrepresentations.

- **Address Environmental Racism:**

Acknowledge and address environmental racism by advocating for clean and safe environments for all communities.

- **Engage in Global Collaboration:**

Recognize that racism is a global issue and collaborate internationally to combat it. Share strategies and support global anti-racism efforts.

- **Empower Youth:**

Encourage young people to become active agents of change through activism and advocacy. Support their involvement in social justice movements.

- **Support Mental Health:**

Provide accessible mental health services and support for individuals affected by racism and discrimination.

- **Participate in Civic Engagement:**

Engage in civic participation, including voting, to promote change and hold elected officials accountable.

- **Economic Equity:**

Advocate for policies and initiatives that promote economic equity, affordable housing, and access to quality jobs for racial minority communities.

- **Challenge Media Bias:**

Develop media literacy skills to critically assess and challenge biased and harmful representations in media and online.

- **Invest in Racial Minority Businesses:**

Support businesses owned by racial minority entrepreneurs and invest in communities that have been historically marginalized.

- **Be an Ally:**

Be an ally to racial minority communities by supporting their causes and advocating for their rights. Listen and learn from their experiences.

The fight against racism is a long-term commitment, and each of us has a role to play in creating a more inclusive and just society. Together, we can challenge discriminatory systems, dismantle racism, and foster a world where all individuals are treated with respect, dignity, and equity, regardless of their race or ethnicity.

Final thoughts

In the complex and ongoing journey to address racism, it's important to remember that every step forward counts, no matter how small. The fight against racism is a collective endeavor, and the journey is marked by both challenges and progress. As we navigate this path, it's crucial to maintain hope and determination.

Understanding the origins of racism, acknowledging its historical context, and exploring the multifaceted factors that perpetuate racial disparities provide us with the knowledge needed to drive meaningful change. These insights guide us toward the creation of a more equitable and just society.

As individuals, communities, and organizations, our shared responsibility is to take action. We must challenge racial bias, support policy reforms, advocate for diversity and inclusion, and actively engage in dismantling discriminatory systems. By listening, learning, and empathizing, we can bridge divides and work together to foster unity and justice.

The journey to a better future free from racism is illuminated by the commitment of people like you. It is a testament to the strength of collective action and the belief that a world where all individuals are treated with respect, dignity, and equity, regardless of their race or ethnicity, is not only possible but essential.

Let our final thoughts be a reaffirmation of our dedication to this cause, a call to action, and a resounding message of hope for a more inclusive and just future.